Eating the Sun

Copyright (c) 2015 by Anna Slesinski

Published by Tea Cup Press
Baltimore, Maryland
All rights reserved.

ISBN-13: 978-0-9962741-1-1

Book Design by Anna Slesinski

Grateful acknowledgement is made to the editors of *Welter* and *The Light Ekphrastic*, where some of these poems, sometimes in earlier versions, first appeared:

Welter: "Waking," "Hypohetical"
The Light Ekphrastic: "Planting," "I am sorry"

*For Mandy —
Can't wait to read
your book next!*

Eating the Sun

Anna Slesinski

Anna Slesinski

Tea Cup Press
Baltimore, Maryland

For my family

*What is taken apart is not utterly demolished.
It is like a great mysterious egg in Kansas*

*that has cracked and hatched two big bewildered birds.
It is two spaceships coming out of retirement,*

*flying away from their dead world,
the burning booster rocket of divorce
                       falling off behind them,*

the bystanders pointing at the sky and saying, Look.

Tony Hoagland

Contents

I
Hold a Breath   1
Ceremony   2
Series of Art School Self-Portraits   4
Traditions   5
Self as Wife   6
I don't   7
Hypothetical   8
Snow Again   9
Couples Therapy   10
Bedroom Audience   11
Sarcasm   12
Waking   13

II
Planting   17
Rebuild   18
Self-Portrait with Dog   19
Pack Castle   20
Viewing   21
All that it entails   22
One Week of Self-Portraits   23
Yesterday   24
Divorced   25
I am sorry   26

III
Rising   31
Acupuncture Self-Portrait   32
Possible   33
Continue to be   34

I

Marriage

*So different, this man
And this woman:
A stream flowing
In a field.*

William Carlos Williams

Hold a Breath

I lie in the bottom
of our pool, the sky a ring.

How did we miss the exit
before this, the one

to warm bed sheets, bright
words smelling like

mint ice cream? I exhale
hot grief and chlorine,

draw it in again.
How am I here?

Ceremony

I.

        take a moment
Please take a

do you   present yourselves

        WE

Will you promise

        WE WILL

Then

II.

you are   my conscience

I promise to always   honest
I promise to sing to you

I am here   to share with you

my sanctuary,
As we start   I vow
               all

to a lifetime of   gardens

III.

I give you this ring   a sign

      to the end
      to the end

      know   I love

IV.

We recognize and

witness.

In accordance with the laws henceforth to be
                a kiss.

Wedding ceremony erasure, August 2010

Series of Art School Self-Portraits

I make myself with charcoal, again with chalk, shadowed
blue, then purple, now oil paint red, woven, each stroke
a new violent skin grown.

They say my nose can't look like that.
I stand next to myself, comparing the planes of my face
to my face. My nose does look like that; I stare at it for hours

to see the shape of it; erasing, erasing, elongate the torso,
sketch the hand behind my head, baring chalk drawn breasts,
bent forward, a green bath towel around my waist, straining
to see my reflection.

Traditions

In the courtyard
between our houses

we keep our ideas
about dying and family;

the ghost of an absent father
paces on the bricks.

When we visit we feed him
imagined memories, touch

the creases in our palms
and marvel at their similarity.

Under the garden bed
we find our own forgotten

children, their brown eyes
pale,

their cupped hands filled with pebbles
they call home.

Self as Wife

The bowl
of my body

held
peach trees

bags of weed
for your herb grinder

your favorite
YouTube videos

car payments and
short cakes

curls of
hard candy

dissolving
into the hard muscle
of your tongue

I don't

I don't
my husband

I have been looking
repeat

keep things private

little

where we are
we have had

terrible awful
possible

August
our   maybe

marriage is

a fire

Journal entry erasure, August 2012

Hypothetical

I start wishing on starfish,
showing my insides to the old neighborhood,

the leaf piles we tossed, chasing each other;
finger tips skimming church room railings;

now we soak together in the lake,
untie aprons, knead selves out of saliva, ribbon,

humility. What if I were a tree –
soft circles stacked together, sap,
knots; could you love a tree?

Snow Again

This winter reminds me
of the year we moved into the house on Abell Avenue,
and I was so depressed I couldn't keep
my eyes open.

I spent evenings in the kitchen writing poems
about flowers, because that was all I wanted
to think about.

My teacher told me it was a lost cause, because
it's impossible to write a poem equal to
a flower.

There was a blizzard too,
the snow so deep and cold that it took
all the color out of the air.

I don't remember much about you being there with me,
except the day we made sugar cookies
and you drew snowmen on them with the icing, because
it was snowing again.

Couples Therapy

Standing in quiet rows, flush
with mosquitoes and gnats, the

green tomatoes roll sweat
down their stalks.

We touch the trellis strings
holding the plants, pluck gently,

talk about our potential harvest
kneeling in the dirt,

the bugs and stones biting our knees.
We point out each green fruit,

our tongues going soft in our mouths,
our hands pulling weeds, testing the soil

for lead, minerals.
We wait for the dirt to start working.

Bedroom Audience

I lie in bed listening to your dishwashing sounds,
the kitchen sink gurgle,

plates click-clicking into the rack
whose feet never sit just right for the water to drain,

making a lake on the counter,
while you watch cartoons

on the table-top TV, laugh,
slide our clean plates into the cabinet,

clatter and converse
with the on-screen characters.

Sarcasm

how   manipulates
       guilt

tantrum
     sarcasm
as   walk in the door.

That was   Wednesday

And when I tried   to say "we can work
     together"

           went on until close to midnight

we ended somewhere
him talking about   freedom

Journal entry erasure, September 2013

Waking

I loved your snores,
that shuddered in your throat and chest

like a black bear grunting, eating jam
snout-deep in the jar – gasp, cough,
quietly start again.

I loved your breath
thick with sleep and spices

dark and musty on the pillow
the smell circling the room
like a possessive animal.

I loved
possessive.

I loved your morning sounds;
you were a rooster,
you'd crow and shake the pillows,

and I'd roll over
pretending I had not woken.

And I loved putting on glasses.
When I wore them

I became Clark Kent. When I took them off again
I became someone else.

I hadn't noticed until
you asked about my secret
identity.

II

Because if marriage is a kind of womb,

divorce is the being born again;
alimony is the placenta one of them will eat;

loneliness is the name of the wet-nurse;
regret is the elementary school;

endurance is the graduation.

Tony Hoagland

Planting

I have lost my curtain.
Sun sits on the wall above my bed,
a yellow square, and I

am round and warm like a seed
listening to the roots rustling
in my skull, light tumbling

down over my bitterest parts
and the city outside. I look out
and see we were never there

yet your face is reflected in the buildings
around me, watching my window
watching the wild things I am planting.

Rebuild

counseling together,   we talked about
                              separation,
                              recovery.

        "how long do I have to be good?"

credit checks and drug testing
        rebuild

I told him I can't   until
        that decision

and I am not   sleeping

I took down   pictures because they are
  crying

Journal entry erasure, September 2013

Self-Portrait with Dog

You are not here. The dog and I keep
looking for you when we hear footsteps on the porch.

We both jump
when the neighbors slam their doors.

Night comes earlier as winter begins.
When the sun sets we sit on the couch.

She growls in her sleep,
pressing her head against my thigh.

The wind blows about our trashcans in the dark,
tosses the wind-chime we bought at the beach.

The kettle shrieks as I make tea, sweep the floor, wash
another dish, pause, listen, see the dog look at the door.

Pack Castle

Fingers black with newspaper ink
smother me in bubbles
and tissue paper, layer me

under cups and saucers,
stolen street signs, books
that might be mine or yours or

do you want the juicer? Folded up
in this cardboard castle, we could
make our new home

with bungee cords to wrap our stiff
contrary chests together, tied tight
so we won't fall off the truck.

Viewing

We walk together through the house
we abandoned

there the brick fireplace we thought would warm us
the bay window that groans when it rains

the kitchen sink full of green water
quiet dishes

dried leaves in the entryway
bird's nest in the tub

the bedroom window we left open a crack thinking
we would be back to close it

we allow ourselves a last look
stunned laughter

nail our grief to the mantel piece
and walk separate ways.

All that it entails

We are less than
          all that it entails.

I am ready for the recovery
I have been making preparations for

nights
to control
          needs,
special food

I keep reassuring myself   I
          know.

      the outcomes are
better than the waiting.

Journal entry erasure, August 2014

One Week of Self-Portraits

Monday I heat up a mug of old coffee
wearing a bathrobe I bought myself as a gift.

Tuesday standing at the café counter,
I listen to elderly women discussing snow.

Wednesday I read emails from my husband,
crying into a bowl of granola.

Thursday driving home from work,
I click through radio commercials.

Friday I read under a wool blanket
on the couch, avoiding the cold walk to bed.

Saturday I undress
in front of an uncovered window.

Sunday in my lover's bed,
our faces close, eyelash to eyelash.

Yesterday

Yesterday,

our hearing
fees paid. Now

wait.

waiting
        it is
our witness,
who died   time ago

in the downpour of rain
that continued all morning.

Journal entry erasure, November 2014

Divorced

Now we are alone again,
and I will continue to sponge away

the imprint of you on every
thing in the house.

The dog does not like it
when I wash her face. She

wags her tail when I say
something that sounds like

your name. Your name
sharp and red in my mouth.

I am sorry

that winter is here, that our season
ended with a sudden frost and plants
dying in their beds

that we are not still in the trees
hanging like green lungs
over the lake

that we are not in the water, our bare legs kicking
crawling onto the rocks
looking up and eating the sun

that the pink blossoms have all died, and that
we could not tell the truth to one another
until now

III

An open door says, "Come in."
A shut door says, "Who are you?"

Carl Sandburg

Rising

We sit, two on an empty beach
hands rubbed together
and between knees to warm. We wait.

Soon other figures appear
along the shore, some in pairs, but each
        apart
quiet

as the sun begins to crest, glowing rose
behind clouds on the water.
Each face lifts, and we watch

the beginning of our mornings, each
an empty bowl on the ocean rim
waiting for the sky to be poured.

Acupuncture Self-Portrait

Needles kiss
      my spine

light falls
through the umbrella tree in the corner.

Leaves
shine like fresh blue
of your eyes

gazing
      kind creases
along the edges,

making me
an envelope

filled with blossoms.

Possible

We drink lemonade from glasses crawling
with buzzing yellow jackets and we repeat our promises
to one another, drink again, again

until we have made a rosary
with our mouths, a rope of intention
and round words like   now
                          and never.

We lick the sweet fear building
in the deep curves of our throats,
each possible happiness
humming against our cheek bones.

Continue to be

I continue to be
        being in love.
     surreal, considering

I could not help but wonder

I did the right thing,

I feel it is coming out of
my body,
        all of this
     glowing

        maybe it is

Journal entry erasure, October 2014

Acknowledgements

Thank you to my teachers – Kendra Kopelke,
Steve Matanle, Pantea Tofangchi, Meredith Purvis,
Valzhyna Mort, and Elizabeth Spires – without whom
I would not be the writer and book arts lover I am today.

And thank you to my classmates – John, Joe, Katrina,
Tim, and Tracy – for their creative input and encouragement.
This book would not be here without all of you.

Thank you to my work colleagues – especially Julie, Robin,
and Erin – for their continuous support while I pursued this
degree.

Thank you to my dear family and friends for their
incredible love and support from my first day of class in
2010 to my graduation in 2015, from newly-wed to
divorced. Thank you for reading rough drafts and telling
me to keep writing.

And thank you to Keith, who cheered me on as I wrote this
book, and who has filled my life with blossoms.

About the Author

Anna Slesinski was born and raised in Baltimore City, and currently lives there with her three-legged dog, DeeDee. She works as the Grants Manager for a local non-profit.

After receiving her high school diploma from the Baltimore School for the Arts, where she was a visual arts major, Anna studied creative writing and studio art at Goucher College. She received her BA from Goucher in 2006, and went on to receive her MFA in creative writing and publishing arts from the University of Baltimore in 2015.

Her poems have been previously published in *Welter* and *The Light Ekphrastic*.

For more information go to:
annaslesinski.wordpress.com.

Colophon

This book was designed by Anna Slesinski. It is set in Gill Sans, a sans-serif typeface designed by Eric Gill in 1926, and Adobe Jenson Pro. Manufactured by Spencer Printing in Honesdale, PA, on 70lb paper.

The cover image is of a "Euphorbia monstrosus" cactus from Madagascar at the Howard Peters Rawlings Conservatory & Botanical Gardens in Baltimore, MD. Photo credit: Anna Slesinski

Printed by Tea Cup Press, Baltimore, MD, 2015.